IN THEIR OWN WORDS

Sojourner Truth

Peter Roop and Connie Roop

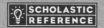

For Joan, a sojourner seeking the truth.
Keep enjoying the journey!

LIBRARY OF CONGRESS CATALOGING-IN-PUBLICATION DATA

Roop, Connie
Sojourner Truth/Connie Roop and Peter Roop
p.   cm.—(In their own words)
Includes bibliographical references and index.
1. Truth, Sojourner, d. 1883—Juvenile literature.   2. African American abolitionists—Biography—Juvenile literature.   3. African American women—Biography—Juvenile literature.   4. Abolitionists—United States—Biography—Juvenile literature.
5. Social reformers—United States—Biography—Juvenile literature.   [1. Truth, Sojourner, d. 1883.   2. Abolitionists.   3. Reformers.   4. African Americans—Biography.   5. Women—Biography.]   I. Roop, Peter.   II. In their own words (Scholastic)
E185.97.T8 R66 2002
305.5′67′092—dc21
[B]   2001032025

ISBN 0-439-26323-9

10 9 8 7 6 5   04 05 06

Composition by Brad Walrod
Printed in the U.S.A.
First printing, February 2002

CONTENTS

INTRODUCTION

IN 1797, ISABELLA HARDENBERGH WAS born a slave. When she died in 1883, Isabella's name was Sojourner Truth. As Sojourner Truth, she died a free woman.

A *sojourner* is a traveler, someone who does not stay long in one place. Isabella's life was a long journey. She was owned by six masters, but mastered by none.

As a child, Isabella spoke Dutch. She spoke English as an adult. She gave speeches to thousands of people throughout the United States. She met presidents Lincoln, Johnson, and Grant. She preached the Bible from memory and sang with a strong voice. She fought for freedom for African Americans and for equal rights for all women.

When Isabella died, a poet said, "Brave, true friend, farewell." A newspaper reporter wrote, "Sojourner Truth was this day honored as none but the great are honored."

At her birth eighty-six years earlier, no one would have guessed the road Sojourner Truth would travel.

The United States was twenty-one years old when Isabella was born. George Washington was president. Every state but Massachusetts allowed slavery. Newspapers were few. Photography had not yet been invented.

During the period of Isabella's life, twenty presidents were elected. The Civil War took place, and slavery was ended. Railroads crossed the country. Photographs became so common, people gave them away. The United States celebrated its 107th birthday.

Isabella loved words. She memorized the Bible and hundreds of songs. She enjoyed speaking before crowds. Her gift of words entertained people and

Sojourner Truth (1797–1883) was a gifted speaker who fought for the rights of African Americans and women.

challenged them. She spoke with wit, wisdom, and energy. She could not read or write, but she told her life story to a friend who wrote it in the book, the *Narrative of Sojourner Truth*. "I can't read a book, but I can read the people," Sojourner said.

We call books like the *Narrative of Sojourner Truth* primary sources. A primary source is an account of events witnessed by a person who was there. Newspaper articles that covered Sojourner Truth's speeches are primary sources. Photographs are, too. Through them we know how she looked, what she wore, and what she said.

We can learn about someone's life through secondary sources, too. A secondary source is a description of a person or an event by someone who was not actually a witness. Encyclopedias are secondary sources. Biographies like this one are also secondary sources. Many primary sources were used to write this biography, but it is not an eyewitness account of Sojourner Truth's life.

By reading Sojourner Truth's own words, you can

sense the power of her speeches. You will discover her intelligence, humor, and determination. You will see what one person did to better the lives of millions.

Now, through many of her own words, journey with Sojourner Truth.

SLAVERY

SOJOURNER TRUTH NEVER KNEW HER birthday. No records were kept of her birth because she was born a slave. This was common. Slaves' birthdays were not written down. Slaves were considered property like cows and horses.

Most likely, Sojourner Truth was born in 1797 near the Hudson River in Ulster County, New York.

Her master was Johannes Hardenbergh, a wealthy landowner. In 1797, few people in New York owned slaves. Johannes Hardenbergh owned seven.

Johannes Hardenbergh fought for American freedom in the Revolutionary War, but he believed in slavery for African Americans.

When Sojourner Truth was born, she was named Isabella. Her last name was Hardenbergh, that of her master. Her parents called her Belle.

Belle's parents, Betsy and James, were both slaves. Belle was their tenth or twelfth child. No one knows exactly how many children they had.

Growing up, Belle knew only her youngest brother, Peter. Her other sisters and brothers had been sold to different owners.

Belle's parents did not speak English. They spoke Dutch, their master's language.

Belle called her mother Mau Mau. This means "Mama" in Dutch. Mau Mau was strong and loving. She worked hard for Mr. Hardenbergh.

Her father, James, was called Baumfree. In Dutch this means "tree." Belle said her father "was very tall and straight, when young," like a tree. Baumfree was hardworking. He cut trees and split logs for firewood. He plowed and planted his master's fields. He dug wells and carried water.

Workdays were long and hard for slaves. Elizabeth Sparks, a slave, explained:

They worked six days from sun to sun. Usually work began when the horn blow and stop when the horn blow. They get off just long enough to eat at noon. Sometimes the men shuck corn till eleven and twelve o'clock at night.

Mau Mau was Baumfree's third wife. His first two wives had been sold to other owners. Belle never knew them.

Belle grew up to be like her parents. She worked hard at her jobs. She was six feet tall with large hands and feet.

But Belle was different. One day she would be free to live life on her own terms.

In 1799, when Belle was two, her master died. Belle and her parents became the property of his son, Charles Hardenbergh.

Charles lived nearby and he owned a few slaves besides Belle and her parents. He ran a busy hotel and a gristmill. Farmers brought their grain to his mill to be ground into flour. He also had a farm

TO BE SOLD,
A likely ſtrong Negro
Girl, abcut 17 Years of Age ; fold
by Reafon that a Boy would fuit
the Owner better. Enquire at
R. & S. Draper's Printing Office

During the eighteenth century, slavery was legal in both the North and the South of the United States. This classified ad for a female slave appeared in a Massachusetts newspaper in 1763.

where Baumfree worked plowing and planting. Mau Mau sewed, cooked, and cleaned.

Using his slaves' labor, Hardenbergh grew and made almost everything he needed. He had chickens, cows, horses, hogs, sheep, and geese. Fish were caught in the river. His slaves cared for his family and the guests at the hotel. They planted and harvested his crops.

Later, Belle said her parents felt Charles Hardenbergh was "the best of the family."

Charles liked Belle's parents. He let them use a little land to grow their own food. After working for

Charles all day, Baumfree, Mau Mau, Peter, and Belle worked on their land in the evenings. They also worked their patch of land on Sundays, a slave's only day off. They grew corn for grinding and flax for thread. Mau Mau traded the corn and flax to Master Hardenbergh for extra clothes and food.

Although Master Hardenbergh liked Belle's family, he did not give them a cabin in which to live. He made his slaves live in the hotel cellar. Men, women, and children slept in this cold, damp, dark room.

Rough boards made an uneven floor. Dirty water dripped down making a muddy mess. Belle remembered "sleeping on those damp boards, like a horse, with a little straw and blanket."

Hardenbergh treated his slaves no better than he treated his animals. Like his animals, they were his property to do with as he pleased.

Life in the cellar was miserable for Belle and the other slaves. They all had sores. Their bones ached from the damp. Coughs and colds were common.

Belle remembered the dark cellar with only a few

panes of thick, dirty glass through which the sun never seemed to shine. The only light came through a pine-knot.

Baumfree and Mau Mau missed their other children. They told stories about them. Belle remembered their heartbreak when she heard about "those dear departed ones, of whom they had been robbed, and for whom their hearts still bled."

Mau Mau would point to stars and say,

Those are the same stars, and that is the same moon, that look down upon your brothers and sisters, and which they see as they look up to them, though they are ever so far away from us and each other.

Through her mother's words and memories, Belle learned about her missing brothers and sisters.

One story, about her brother Michael and sister Nancy, stayed with Belle all her life. It happened one snowy winter day. Michael was five years old and Nancy was three. Belle had not yet been born. She listened to her parents tell the sad tale.

Slaves were often sold away from their families at slave auctions such as this one.

That terrible morning Michael got up "with the birds, kindled a fire, calling for his Mau Mau to 'come, for all was now ready for her.'"

Steaming horses pulled a sleigh over the snow-covered ground. It stopped at Colonel Hardenbergh's house. Michael ran to the sleigh. He was picked up and put in. Michael thought he was going on a sleigh ride!

Little Nancy was also carried to the sleigh. Michael was surprised when she was not placed beside him. Instead, she was put into a box and the box was locked!

Michael understood what was happening. "Like a frightened deer he sprang from the sleigh, and running into the house, concealed himself under a bed."

His hiding place was discovered. He was carried struggling to the sleigh. With a snap of the whip, the driver started the horses. Michael and Nancy were taken away to be sold to another master. Mau Mau and Baumfree never saw them again.

Charles Crawley, a slave, said, "Lord! Lord! I done seen them younguns fight and kick like crazy folks. Child, it was pitiful to watch them [be sold away]."

Later, when Belle's own son, Peter, was sold into slavery in the South, she would fight back. She would not let what happened to Michael and Nancy happen to her son!

CHILDHOOD

MAU MAU AND BAUMFREE WERE loving, but strict, with Belle and Peter. They never knew when they or their children might be sold away, so they taught them the best they could.

Even though they were children, as slaves, Belle and Peter chopped wood and hoed the garden. They fed the chickens and milked the cows. They helped in the hotel and worked in the fields.

Like many slaves, Mau Mau was a firm believer in God. Mau Mau taught Belle to say the Lord's Prayer. In the evenings, Mau Mau sat with Belle and Peter. She told them about "the only Being that could...aid or protect them."

"My children, there is a God, who hears and sees you," Mau Mau said.

"A God, Mau Mau! Where does he live?" asked the children.

"He lives in the sky," Mau Mau said. "And when you are beaten, or cruelly treated, or fall into any trouble, you must ask help of Him, and He will always hear and help you."

Mau Mau taught Belle and Peter to be honest, to obey their masters, and not to steal.

Belle helped Mau Mau take care of her father. Baumfree was older than Mau Mau. The long days in the fields had stolen his strength. The cold, damp cellar had robbed him of his health. Baumfree was no longer the tall, straight tree for which he was named. Instead, he was stooped, weak, and aching.

In 1806, Belle's life changed forever. Master Charles died.

Charles Hardenbergh's possessions were counted. He owned "21 chairs, 4 axes, 1 waggon, 1 windmill, 13 sheep and 5 lambs, 8 hogs, 1 plow, 5 geese,

5 cows, [and] 8 chickens." He owned tools, a spinning wheel, and many other things.

And he owned slaves. They were listed as "1 Negro Wench [woman] Bett [Mau Mau], 1 D [daughter] Isabella, 1 Boy Peet [Peter]."

Hardenbergh's list gave the value of his slaves. "Bett, $1. Peet, $100. Isabella, $100."

The "slaves, horses, and other cattle" of Charles Hardenbergh were sold in an auction. Whoever offered the most money would own them.

Robert Williams, a slave, said this about an auction he watched when he was a boy: "The block was a big rock that slaves would stand on so they would be over the crowd. The seller would cry bids, '$150, who will make it $160?'"

Belle, Peter, and Mau Mau were to be sold. Then one of the Hardenbergh relatives asked, "Who shall be burdened with Baumfree, when we have sent away his faithful Mau Mau Bett?"

None of the relatives wanted the old man. He was too worn out to work so they could not sell him. He was crippled and going blind. They would have to

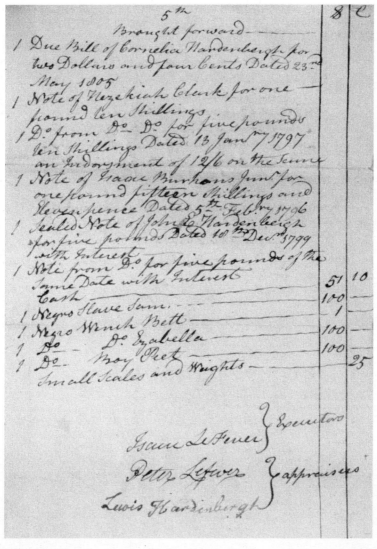

This page lists some of Charles Hardenbergh's property, including Isabella and her family.

feed and care for him until he died. Baumfree was worth so little money he was not even on the list of Hardenbergh's possessions.

No one would take Baumfree. So the Hardenberghs decided not to sell Mau Mau. She would be given her freedom to take care of Baumfree. This pleased the husband and wife for they would still be together.

But their last two children would be torn away.

Peter was quickly sold to a new master.

But no one would buy the tall, skinny Belle. Finally, Hardenbergh's sheep (value $25) were added to the sale.

John Neely paid $100 for the sheep and Belle. Neely owned a store in the nearby town of Kingston, New York. Belle was nine years old and had a new master. Her parents could not help her anymore. She would have to face the world by herself.

What would her life with the Neelys be like? Belle worried.

ALONE

WHEN BELLE LEFT HER PARENTS for the Neelys, she was angry and upset. Later she said, after Mr. Neely bought her, "Now the war begun."

Belle worried about her parents. Even though she was only nine, she could do many things to make their lives easier. She was especially concerned about frail Baumfree.

Belle took comfort that her parents were together. They depended on each other. Mau Mau worked to earn a little money. She cooked and cared for Baumfree.

Baumfree did odd jobs to earn pennies. Kind neighbors helped them, too.

Their lives were miserable, though. Mau Mau

and Baumfree continued living in the damp hotel cellar. They gathered fruit and grew some food, but struggled to find enough to eat.

Occasionally, Mr. Neely let Belle visit her parents. She saw them four times with months between visits. When Belle was eleven, Mau Mau died.

One cool fall day, Mau Mau told Baumfree she was going to bake bread. He said he would knock "some apples from a tree. If she could get some of them baked with the bread, it would give it a nice relish [treat] for the dinner."

Baumfree knocked the apples down and saw "Mau Mau come out and gather them up."

Baumfree raked for a neighbor, then came home for dinner. Climbing down into the cellar, he expected to smell fresh bread and cooked apples. Instead, as he felt around blindly, he found Mau Mau lying on the dirty floor. He lifted her onto their mattress and cared for her the best he could. Mau Mau died a few hours later.

Their new masters let Peter and Belle go to their

mother's burial. They could not stay long, however. They had to return to work.

Belle said she could still hear her father forty years later. "I HEAR it *now*—and remember it as well as yesterday— *poor old man!!!*"

Baumfree cried, "I had thought God would take me first. Mau Mau was so much smarter than I and could get about and take care of herself. I am so *old* and so *helpless*."

Belle and Peter returned to their masters. Baumfree was alone. The Hardenberghs,

Life was often difficult for elderly slaves. Once they were too frail to work, they held little value for their owners.

however, took pity on their faithful slave, "permitting him to stay a few weeks at one house, and then a while at another, and so around."

Belle begged Mr. Neely for permission to visit her lonely father. Only twice was she allowed to see him. The last time Belle saw Baumfree he was sitting on a rock miles from his home. His hair was as white as wool, he was blind, and his walk "was more a creep than a walk."

Together they walked slowly to his cold cellar.

Belle promised to take care of him "as Mau Mau would if she was here." She told him that the slaves in New York would be freed in ten years.

"Oh, my child," Baumfree told his daughter. "I cannot *live* that long."

When Belle left, she willed her father to keep living. "As I ever thought anything in my life . . . I insisted on his living."

Even Belle's strong will could not keep her father alive. Baumfree soon died.

Belle was truly alone. All her family had died or been sold away. She had only the Neelys to turn to and she found little comfort there. John Neely was busy with his store. Belle spent her time helping Mrs. Neely. Mrs. Neely spoke English, not Dutch, which Belle spoke. This led to many misunderstandings.

Belle described it this way: "If they sent me for a frying pan, not knowing what they meant, perhaps I carried them the pot hooks... then, oh! how angry mistress would be with me!" Belle was yelled at, sometimes even beaten.

Delia Garlic, a slave, said, "It's bad to belong to folks that own you soul and body; that can tie you up to a tree... who take a long curling whip and cut blood with every lick."

In winter, things were worse for Belle. She had large feet. The Neelys gave her little to cover them. As a result, Belle's feet became badly frozen. She suffered "*terribly, terribly*" from the cold.

One Sunday Belle was given a horrible beating. Master Neely told her to go to the barn. Belle did not know what she had done wrong. Had she angered Mrs. Neely again? she wondered.

KNOW all Men by these Presents,
THAT I *Johannes Doxstedder of*
Burnetsfield In the County of Albany
For and in Consideration of the Sum of *Ninety Pounes*
Current Money of the Province of
New York to me in Hand paid at and before the Ensealing
and Delivery of these Presents, by *Jacob Cuyler*
of the City of Albany the Receipt whereof I do hereby
acknowledge, and myself to be therewith fully satisfied, contented, and
paid: HAVE Granted, Bargained, Sold, Released, and by these Presents
do fully, clearly and absolutely grant, bargin, sell and releafe unto the

Said Jacob Cuyler a negro Named
Har about Eighteen years old
To HAVE and to HOLD, the said *Negro Nam'd Har*
unto the said *Jacob Huyler His Eyres*
Executors, Administrators, and Assigns, for ever And I the said
Jh Dxstedder for my Self, my Heirs, Executors and Administrators,
do covenant and agree to and with the above-named *Jacob Cuyler*
His Executors, Administrators and Assigns, to
warrant and defend the Sale of the above-named *Negro Har*
against all Persons whatsoever. IN WITNESS
whereof I have hereunto set my Hand and Seal, this *Twelveth*
Day of *October* Annoq. Dom. One Tousand Seven Hundred
~~and Fifty~~ *Sixty three*

Sealed and Delivered in
the Presence of

George Smith

Slaves were considered property and could be sold whenever a slave
owner chose. This bill of sale is for an eighteen-year-old male slave in
New York. It is dated October 12, 1763.

Mr. Neely tied her hands and gave her the worst beating of her life. Belle carried the scars of that beating to her grave.

Later in her life, Belle said, "And now I hear 'em tell of whipping women on bare flesh, it makes *my* flesh crawl and my very hair rise on my head!" She added, "What a way is this of treating human beings?"

In her hours of hardship, Belle remembered Mau Mau's advice to trust God. She did not know that people sometimes pray silently, however. Belle believed God heard her prayers only if she prayed out loud. This was hard to do when people were around, especially her master.

One day a man named Mr. Schriver asked Belle if she would like to work for him. He ran a tavern six miles away and needed help. Belle, thinking her prayers had been answered, agreed.

Mr. Neely, tired of his wife's bad temper, agreed to sell Belle to Mr. Schriver for $105.

Mr. Schriver ran his tavern and fished to make extra money. He had a farm but let most of it grow wild.

Belle did just about everything for the Schrivers. She carried the heavy fish her master caught. She hoed his corn patch and planted seeds. She found roots and herbs in the forests. She walked to town to buy supplies.

This hard work and outdoor life was better for Belle. The Schrivers were not educated and their language was bad, but they did not beat her. She was not afraid of her new master as she had been with Mr. Neely.

In 1810, Belle's life journey reached another turn. She was thirteen and was sold again. Her new owner would be her fifth master.

This time, Mr. John Dumont, a farmer, bought Belle. For the next sixteen years, until she was about thirty years old, Belle was a Dumont slave.

MARRIAGE

MR. DUMONT AND HIS FAMILY lived nearby in New Paltz, New York. Here Belle learned to speak English for the first time.

Mr. Dumont owned four slaves. He was usually a kind master to Belle. Once, however, he beat her. Mr. Dumont appreciated how hard Belle worked plowing, planting, hoeing, and harvesting. He said, "She could do as much work as half a dozen common people."

Such praise made others jealous of Belle.

Mrs. Dumont had a strong dislike for Belle and she thought Belle did poor work. She believed Belle's work "came from her hand half performed."

Mrs. Dumont hired two white girls to help her.

One girl, Kate, was mean to Belle and she took every chance "to grind her down." Kate wanted Belle to look bad to Mrs. Dumont.

One day Mrs. Dumont asked Belle to cook potatoes for breakfast. Belle scrubbed the potatoes, put them into the iron kettle, added fuel to the fire, and went on to her next task.

When Belle's back was turned, Kate grabbed a handful of dirt and threw it into the boiling potatoes.

Upon opening the lid, Belle saw "the potatoes [she] cooked for breakfast assumed a dingy, dirty look."

Mrs. Dumont "blamed her severely." She told Mr. Dumont that the potatoes were "a fine specimen of Belle's work! . . . It is the the way *all* her work is done."

Mr. Dumont scolded Belle and "commanded her to be more careful in the future." Belle promised she would. But she was puzzled. Why had the potatoes looked so bad?

Kate laughed. She didn't tell Belle she had added the dirt to the potatoes.

Gertrude, a Dumont daughter, felt sorry for Belle.

Some slaves, like this young man from New York, worked in their masters' homes rather than working outdoors. Belle began working in the Dumont household in 1810.

She was ten years old, "a good, kind-hearted girl." She offered to help Belle.

Gertrude said, "They would see if they could not have them [the potatoes] *nice* and not have Poppee and Matty [her parents], and all of 'em, scolding so terribly."

Belle accepted Gertrude's kind offer. The next

morning, while Belle milked the cow, Gertrude watched the potatoes.

Gertrude watched as Kate "sweeping about the fire, caught up a chip, lifted some ashes with it, and dashed them into the kettle. Now the mystery was solved, the plot discovered!"

Gertrude told her parents that Kate was spoiling the potatoes. "I saw her do it! . . . Look at those [ashes] that fell on the outside of the kettle. You can now see what made the potatoes so dingy every morning, though Belle washed them clean."

Mrs. Dumont said nothing. Kate "looked like a convicted criminal."

After this, Belle worked harder to please Mr. Dumont. He bragged to his friends that Belle "is better to me than a *man*—for she will do a good family's washing in the night, and be raking and binding [tying up hay] as my best hands [hired helpers]" in the morning.

Belle worked even harder when she heard this praise. Some nights she would not lie down to sleep, but took cat naps in a chair. Her efforts pleased Mr. Dumont.

While Belle was still a slave, she met Robert, another slave. Robert lived on a nearby farm. Belle and Robert fell in love and wished to be married.

Robert's owner, Charles Catton, said Robert could not marry Belle. He wanted Robert to marry one of his slaves so their children would belong to him.

Robert wanted Belle to be his wife. He slipped away to see her whenever he could. He did not think his master knew he was visiting Belle.

Mr. Catton made a plan to catch Robert at Belle's cabin. One Saturday Mr. Catton told a slave that Belle was sick. When Robert heard this, he went to see her. It was a trap!

Mr. Catton and his son caught Robert. Belle, watching from a window, described it this way. "They both fell upon him like tigers, beating him with the heavy ends of their canes."

Mr. Dumont rushed to Robert's aid. Dumont told

the Cattons "they could no longer thus spill human blood" on his land.

The Cattons tied Robert's hands behind him. Mr. Dumont made them loosen the knots. He followed the Cattons and Robert home to make sure Robert was not hurt anymore.

Belle, who had loved Robert, never saw him again. She never found out what happened to him after that terrible last visit.

Even though Mr. Dumont had helped Belle, he made her marry Tom, one of his slaves. Tom had been married twice before, but his wives had been sold away. As slaves, Belle and Tom had no choice but to obey their master. They were married in about 1815 when Belle was about nineteen years old.

The state of New York did not recognize slave marriages as legal, so Tom and Belle were not married by a minister. They were married with "one of the slaves performing the ceremony for them."

Elizabeth Sparks, a Virginia slave, was married in 1861. She was nineteen like Belle. She said, "I got permission to get married. You always had to get

Slave couples, like this one in the South in the 1800s, were married at a ceremony in which they jumped over a broom together.

permission. You jump across a broomstick together, and you was married."

Belle and Tom had five children. Diana was born about 1815 and Peter, her only son, about 1820. Elizabeth was born about 1825 and Sophia in 1826. One other baby did not live long enough to be named.

When Belle worked in the fields, she took her

children with her. She put the youngest child in a handmade basket and hung the basket from a branch. An older child would swing the basket to keep the baby happy while Belle worked.

When the children were old enough, they chopped wood, carried water, and worked in the garden and the fields. Diana, Belle's oldest daughter, remembered the long days working at a man's tasks: plowing, planting, and hoeing corn and wheat; pulling flax; picking rocks out of the stony fields; spinning wool; and dozens of other jobs.

Belle was strict with her children, just as her mother had been with her. When they were hungry, she wouldn't let them steal. She said, "The Lord only knows how many times I let my children go hungry rather than take secretly the bread I liked not to ask for."

Mr. Dumont was kind to Belle as she raised her children. If he found a child crying while Belle was working, he spoke up. He said, "I will not hear any child cry so. Here Belle, take care of this child, if no more work is done for a week."

Mrs. Dumont disagreed. She never liked Belle. But she said nothing because she did not want to make her husband angry.

In 1824, the state of New York passed a law to free slaves gradually within its borders. Slaves who had worked for twenty years would be set free on July 4, 1827.

That meant Belle would be freed on July 4, 1827! Later, her children would be freed, too. Under the law, Diana would be freed in 1840, Peter in 1849, Elizabeth in 1850, and baby Sophia in 1851.

Mr. Dumont had been pleased with Belle's hard work. He promised her that "if she would do well, and be faithful, he would give her 'free papers' one year before" he had to.

On July 4, 1826, Belle would be a free woman.

FREEDOM

BELLE BELIEVED MR. DUMONT. SHE had worked hard before, but now she turned to her tasks with increased energy.

She worked in the fields, plowing, planting, hoeing, harvesting. She was an expert in tying the corn stalks into bundles, called sheafs. Belle would "bind a sheaf, throw it up in the air, and have another one bound before the other fell."

Belle cooked, cleaned, ironed and mended clothes, and spun wool.

She raised her four children, teaching them about God, honesty, and hard work. She nursed them when they were sick and cheered them up when they were sad.

When Diana was older, she remembered her mother's stories and dream of freedom.

Diana said Belle "used to sit with her children on the floor in their cabin on the Dumont farm, before a fire place, with a pine-knot for a light, and mend her clothing, and talk with them."

Belle shared her dreams of freedom and owning her own home. Diana remembered, "She told the children that some day they would have a home of their own, and that the family would all be together."

Diana went to school once. She said she "was sent to school for just one week, but had no idea what the school was for, or why she was sent there." She added, "The school teacher never spoke" to her the whole week. She did not learn how to read. Diana was probably sent to school so the Dumonts could say they tried to obey the law.

Belle never did learn to read. Whenever she could, she listened to someone read the Bible. Her memory was good, and she learned many parts of the

Bible just by listening. Belle's daughters, Sophia, Diana, and Elizabeth, did not learn how to read either. When he was older, her son, Peter, learned to read and write.

Even though Belle could not read, she loved to sing. She sang while working and sang for pleasure. Gertrude Dumont remembered Belle as having "a rich and powerful" voice. When Belle heard a song she liked, she memorized it.

One day in 1825, while working in the fields, Belle cut her right hand. She bravely bandaged the wound and kept working. But the injury was serious. She could not work as hard as she did before. Belle's hand never recovered. Her crippled fingers can be seen in photographs of her taken thirty-five years later.

When July 4, 1826, came, Mr. Dumont refused to free Belle. He claimed that because her hand was hurt, she had not done enough work. Instead of admitting he had broken his promise, he said Belle had broken hers!

Later Belle said, "The slaveholders are TERRIBLE for

promising to give you this or that...if you will do thus and so. When...one claims the promise, they ...recollect nothing of the kind."

To make matters worse, Mr. Dumont sold Belle's five-year-old son, Peter, to a neighbor named Dr. Gedney. Dr. Gedney took Peter to New York City. Peter would be Dr. Gedney's servant there.

Belle couldn't help Peter, but she could help herself. She quietly made a plan. No matter what, Mr. Dumont had to free her on July 4, 1827. She would meet him halfway. To be fair, she would spin Dumont 100 pounds of wool. When the wool was spun, she would leave. It would take her six months to spin the wool. She would work those six months and then run away.

Belle worked hard all that summer and fall. After putting in a long day in the fields, she would clean, card, and spin wool late into the night. Her injured hand slowed her down, but she never gave up.

Fall became winter. Belle worried, "How can I get away?" She also wondered how she could take her children.

Slave owners often sent dogs out to search for runaway slaves. This was just one of the risks runaways faced.

She prayed to God. She "told God she was afraid to go in the night, and in the day everybody would see her."

Then she had an idea. "She could leave just before the day dawned, and get out of the neighborhood where she was known before people were much astir."

Belle thanked God saying, "Thank you, God, for *that* thought!"

Early one morning Belle packed. The food she took and her extra clothes filled one cotton handkerchief. She told no one her plans, not even her husband, Tom.

Belle was torn about her children. She couldn't take them all with her. She would take infant Sophia because she was too young to be left behind. Diana and Elizabeth would stay with Tom.

With Sophia on her hip and her belongings in her handkerchief, Belle stepped out of her cabin.

She was free!

Belle walked as fast as she could. High on a hilltop, the sun shone on the mother and child. Belle felt that the sun had never before been so strong and bright. She didn't see anyone chasing her, so she sat down on a rock. "Where, and to whom, shall I go?" she asked herself. In her hurry to escape, Belle had not planned where she would go. She prayed for God's help.

Suddenly, she remembered a man named Levi

Rowe. Mr. Rowe lived in the direction she was traveling. Maybe he would help her.

Belle and Sophia hurried the five miles to his house. Mr. Rowe told her to go to Isaac and Maria Van Wagenen. The Van Wagenens did not believe in slavery. They would protect Belle and Sophia, even if Mr. Dumont found them.

The Van Wagenens greeted her warmly. They never turned away anyone needy. They offered Belle a place to stay and work to do. Belle would finally be paid for her hard work!

Mr. Dumont discovered where Belle was. He rode over to the Van Wagenens' to bring her back. He said, "Well, Belle, so you've run away from me."

Belle replied, "No, I did not *run* away. I walked away by daylight, and all because you had promised me a year of my time."

Mr. Dumont said, "You must go back with me."

Belle said, "No, I *won't* go back with you."

"Well, I shall take the child," Dumont stated.

Mr. Van Wagenen offered to buy Belle's services "for the balance of the year."

RUN away, on the 3d Day of *May* laft, a young Negro Boy, named *Joe*, this Country born, formerly be longed to Capt. *Hugh Hest.* Whoever brings the faid Boy the Subfcriber at *Edifto*, or to the Work Houfe in *Charles Town*, fhall have 3 *l* reward. On the contrary who-ever harbours the faid Boy, may depend upon being feverely profecuted, by
Thomas Chifham.

NOTICE OF RUNAWAY SLAVE. "CHARLESTON GAZETTE," 1744.

Slave owners posted notices and offered rewards in the hope of having their runaway slaves returned. This notice about a runaway slave boy appeared in a Charleston, South Carolina, newspaper.

Mr. Dumont, knowing Belle would soon be free anyway, charged $20 for Belle and $5 for Sophia.

Belle lived with the Van Wagenens for a year. She cooked, cleaned, washed, and ironed. She cared for the vegetable garden and tended the animals.

Belle and baby Sophia had a small room of their own. They even had a clean straw mattress.

On July 4, 1827, New York freed all slaves aged twenty-eight or older. There was little news in the papers about it. White New Yorkers held no celebrations.

For many African-American New Yorkers, though, this was Freedom Day!

The law stated that Sophia had to work for no pay until she was twenty-five years old. To celebrate Freedom Day, the Van Wagenens freed Sophia, too.

Belle decided to change her name. She had been born Isabella Hardenbergh. She had to take Hardenbergh because that was her master's name.

Now she chose to be Isabella Van Wagenen.

Isabella missed her two girls back at the Dumonts. She worried about Peter.

That year Isabella learned some terrible news.

Peter was too small to do the jobs Dr. Gedney wanted him to do. So he gave Peter to his brother, Solomon Gedney.

Solomon Gedney sold Peter to Mr. Fowler, a rich Alabama planter who had just married Solomon's daughter, Liza. The Fowlers took Peter to Alabama.

Solomon Gedney knew it was against the law to sell a slave to a Southern owner, but he sold Peter anyway.

Isabella was determined to get her son back. She knew Mr. Gedney had broken the law. Isabella Van Wagenen set out to rescue Peter.

THE FIGHT
FOR PETER

OW COULD A BLACK WOMAN challenge a white man? Isabella wondered. She could not read or write. She had no money.

But she was free. Free to come and go as she chose. Free to talk with others. Free to find her son.

Isabella took action. She left Sophia with the Van Wagenens. She walked to the Dumonts. Isabella approached her old enemy, Mrs. Dumont. She told her what had happened to Peter.

Mrs. Dumont snorted, "*Ugh!* A fine mess to make about a little [boy]."

Isabella said, "*I'll have my child again.*"

Mrs. Dumont laughed. "Have your child again! How can you get him? Have you any money?"

With iron in her voice, Isabella stated, "I have no money, but God has enough, or what's better! And I'll have my child again."

When Isabella left, she felt different. "Why, I felt so *tall within*—I felt as if the power of a nation was with me!"

Isabella went to Mrs. Gedney. Her daughter, Liza, had married Mr. Fowler, Peter's new master.

Isabella begged for Peter's return. "I'll have my child again," she said.

Mrs. Gedney was as hard-hearted as Mrs. Dumont. She laughed in Isabella's face. "Dear me! What is *your* child, better than *my* child? [Liza] is gone out there, and yours is gone to live with her, to have enough of everything, and to be treated like a gentleman!"

Isabella said, "Yes, your child has gone there, but she is *married* and my boy has gone as a *slave*." She added sadly, "He is too little to go so far from his mother. Oh, I must have my child."

Mrs. Gedney only laughed harder.

Isabella left. To whom could she turn for help now? Wearily, she sat down by the roadside.

Isabella "begged of God that He would show to those about her that He was her helper."

Soon Isabella met a kind man who was an abolitionist. Abolitionists fought against slavery. Some helped slaves escape from their owners. Others wrote and spoke against the evils of slavery.

The man told Isabella to see a peaceful Quaker family who were against slavery. The family welcomed her and listened to her story. They gave her supper and a "nice, high, clean, white, *beautiful* bed" stuffed with soft feathers.

Isabella had never slept in a real bed before. She had only slept on floors or straw mattresses. Isabella was uneasy about lying on the bed so she lay on the floor underneath it!

Then Isabella had a thought. She did not want to hurt the family's feelings by not sleeping in the offered bed. Weary with worry about Peter and hopeful that something might be done, she climbed into the "*beautiful* bed" and fell asleep.

The Ulster County Courthouse in Kingston, New York, still stands today. A plaque outside the courthouse honors Sojourner Truth.

The Quaker family took Isabella to Kingston, New York, to the Ulster County Courthouse. They told her to "enter a complaint to the Grand Jury." The Grand Jury was a group of men who made sure people followed the county laws.

Isabella's hopes soared. With the help of the law, she would get Peter back.

Isabella entered the courthouse. In her deep, strong voice, she told the Grand Jury how Peter had been sold to an owner in the South. She knew it was against the law.

Mr. Charles Chip, a clerk, asked Isabella "if she could *swear* that the child she spoke of was her son?"

Isabella said firmly, "I *swear* it's my son."

Mr. Chip gave Isabella a writ, a paper stating that Peter had to be returned to New York. She must give the writ to the constable, a law officer, in New Paltz. He would take it to Solomon Gedney.

Isabella began "trotting" the nine miles to New Paltz.

The constable made a mistake. He gave the writ to the wrong Gedney, one of Solomon's other brothers.

When he learned the constable was after him, Solomon Gedney went to a lawyer. The lawyer told him to "go to Alabama and bring back the boy." If he didn't, Gedney would be put in jail for fourteen years and be fined $1,000.

That summer of 1828 Isabella moved to Kingston to be closer to the court. Mr. Dumont, her old master, had forgiven her. He let Sophia live with her sisters on his farm.

Isabella learned that Solomon Gedney had secretly traveled south. Travel was difficult in 1828. There were no trains or steamboats to take him straight to Alabama. It wasn't until the spring of 1829 that Solomon Gedney returned, but he wasn't alone. Peter was with him!

Isabella was overjoyed. Peter was back in New York. Now she wanted him to be set free. Solomon Gedney refused. He said Peter was his property. He would not free him.

Isabella went to Herman M. Romeyn, another lawyer. He said, "If she would give him five dollars, he would get her son for her, in twenty-four hours."

"Why," Isabella replied, "I have no *money*, and never had a dollar in my life!"

Mr. Romeyn said, "If you will go to those Quakers in Poppletown [who had taken her to the courthouse], they will help you to [find] five dollars in cash."

This view of Ulster County, New York, was painted by a local artist during the time Isabella lived there.

Isabella marched the ten miles to Poppletown. The Quakers gave her more than the five dollars she needed. Isabella swiftly returned to Kingston and gave Mr. Romeyn all the money.

Friends told her she was foolish to give all the money to the lawyer. She should have kept some to buy herself shoes and clothes.

Isabella answered, "Oh, I do not want the money

and clothes now. I only want my son. And if five dollars will get him, more will *surely* get him."

Mr. Romeyn kept his promise. Within twenty-four hours, Solomon Gedney brought Peter to town.

Mr. Romeyn took Isabella to see her son. When he saw his mother, Peter "cried . . . and [saw] her as some terrible being who was about to take him away from a kind and loving friend."

What had happened to her beloved Peter? she wondered.

Peter "begged them, with tears, not to take him away from his dear master, who had brought [him] from the dreadful South, and been so kind to him."

Isabella saw a scar on Peter's head.

Peter said that Mr. Fowler's horse had kicked him.

When asked about a scar on his cheek, he answered, "That was done by running against the carriage."

Isabella patiently waited for Peter to calm down, talking gently to him.

As last he said, "Well, you *do* look like my mother *used* to."

Isabella hugged him and lifted his shirt. Whip marks covered his back!

"Heavens! What is all this?" she asked.

Peter answered, "It is where Fowler whipped, kicked, and beat me."

Isabella held her sobbing son and comforted him. He knew this was his mother.

With her victory in getting Peter back, Isabella Van Wagenen became the first African-American woman to win a lawsuit in the United States.

Now Isabella and Peter could make a new life together.

CHAPTER 8

NEW LIFE IN NEW YORK

L IFE WAS CHANGING FOR AFRICAN Americans in New York. Since many were no longer slaves, local farmers had to pay for their labor. Most farmers turned to their families to help out because relatives would not have to be paid.

Many African-American workers looked elsewhere for work. Some helped dig the Erie Canal connecting the Hudson River with Lake Erie. Others moved to New York City where there was plenty of work.

In 1829, Isabella decided that she and Peter would move to New York City.

New York City was eighty miles away down the

Hudson. Isabella had no money to make the long journey.

Then Isabella met someone who changed her life. This time it was Miss Gear, who taught in New York City. Miss Gear invited Isabella and Peter to come to New York. She told Isabella that she could easily find housework that would pay her twice what she was being paid then. Peter could go to school, too. Miss Gear offered to pay for their passage by boat to New York.

Ever since her children had been little, Isabella had dreamed of owning her own home and having her family with her. Maybe moving to New York City would make this dream come true.

Isabella accepted Miss Gear's offer. She packed her few belongings in a pillowcase and laced up her new shoes, the first she had ever owned. With Peter in tow, Isabella set forth for New York.

As someone who had grown up in the country, Isabella was shocked by the hustle of New York City. Ships lined the wharves. Buildings, three and four stories tall, towered above. Horses, carts, and

More than 200,000 people lived in New York City when Isabella arrived there in 1829. This painting shows what the Wall Street area of the city looked like in the 1830s.

carriages filled the streets. Church spires stretched toward the sky. People hurried to work and play.

Isabella worked hard scrubbing floors, washing clothes, and cooking meals. She earned enough money to open a bank account. Maybe someday she really would own her own house!

Isabella joined the Zion Methodist Church, which

had mostly black worshippers. She prayed, preached, and sang there. She was so enthusiastic about her church that she convinced others to join it.

Not long after she moved to New York City, Isabella accidentally met her older sister, Sophia. In fact, Isabella had named her youngest daughter after this sister she had never known.

As they talked, Isabella and Sophia realized they were related!

Sophia told Isabella some astonishing news. Their brother Michael also lived in New York! Isabella knew Michael only through their mother's story about his being taken away in a sleigh.

Isabella, Michael, and Sophia had a tearful reunion. Isabella told them she attended Zion Methodist Church. Michael said that was where another sister, Nancy, had also worshipped. Unfortunately, Nancy had just died. Michael described Nancy. She was the small girl who had been placed in the locked box on the sleigh!

Suddenly, Isabella realized that she knew Nancy from church. But she had not known that Nancy was her older sister.

Isabella said, "We met, and was I not, at the time, struck with the peculiar feeling of her hand—the bony hardness so just like mine? And yet I could not know she was my sister. Now I see she looked so like my mother!"

Isabella cried out, "Oh Lord, what is this slavery, that it can do such dreadful things? What evil can it not do?"

For the first time in many years Isabella had family near: her son, Peter, and now Sophia and Michael. Isabella felt that her decision to move to New York had been a good one.

On Sunday afternoons Isabella helped poor young women at the Magdalene Asylum. The asylum provided food and shelter to homeless girls of all races. Isabella taught them sewing, washing, cleaning, and ironing skills so they could get jobs.

Sometimes, Isabella went with Elijah Pierson, the asylum's director, to find homeless girls who needed help. Through Mr. Pierson, Isabella met a very religious man named Robert Matthews.

Mr. Matthews called himself Matthias after a figure in the Bible. He believed God told him to make the world perfect. His followers prayed, exercised, and took cold baths. They ate fruits, vegetables, and little meat.

In 1832, Matthias moved to New York City. Mr. Pierson and Isabella became devoted followers of Matthias. When he suggested that their group move to Zion Hill, New York, Isabella and Pierson followed him. As hard as it was, Isabella left Peter in New York City with friends.

This would be a difficult time in Isabella's life. Although Matthias preached against slavery, he made Isabella do all his housework for free. Sometimes he even beat her. Yet Isabella trusted him. She was taken in by his charm. She even gave Matthias money from her savings.

Other people felt Matthias was tricking Isabella. They told her to leave Matthias. She refused.

In 1834, Mr. Pierson got sick. Matthias would not let a doctor care for him. In August, Elijah Pierson died.

Matthias was accused of killing him. Isabella spoke up for Matthias in court. She gave him the rest of her money to pay his legal bills.

DECLARATION OF THE ANTI-SLAVERY CONVENTION.

ASSEMBLED IN PHILADELPHIA, DECEMBER 4, 1833.

THE Convention assembled in the city of Philadelphia to organize a National Anti-Slavery Society, promptly seize the opportunity to promulgate the following DECLARATION OF SENTIMENTS, as cherished by them in relation to the enslavement of one-sixth portion of the American people.

More than fifty-seven years have elapsed since a band of patriots convened in this place, to devise measures for the deliverance of this country from a foreign yoke. The corner-stone upon which they founded the Temple of Freedom was broadly this—"that all men are created equal; that they are endowed by their Creator with certain inalienable rights; that among these are life, LIBERTY, and the pursuit of happiness." At the sound of their trumpet-call, three millions of people rose up as from the sleep of death, and rushed to the strife of blood; deeming it more glorious to die instantly as freemen, than desirable to live one hour as slaves. They were few in number—poor in resources; but the honest conviction that Truth, Justice, and Right were on their side, made them invincible.

We have met together for the achievement of an enterprise, without which, that of our fathers is incomplete; and which, for its magnitude, solemnity, and probable results upon the destiny of the world, as far transcends theirs, as moral truth does physical force.

In purity of motive, in earnestness of zeal, in decision of purpose, in intrepidity of action, in steadfastness of faith, in sincerity of spirit, we would not be inferior to them.

Their principles led them to wage war against their oppressors, and to spill human blood like water, in order to be free. *Ours* forbid the doing of evil that good may come, and lead us to reject, and to entreat the oppressed to reject, the use of all carnal weapons for deliverance from bondage; relying solely upon those which are spiritual, and mighty through God to the pulling down of strong holds.

Their measures were physical resistance—the marshalling in arms—the hostile array—the mortal encounter. *Ours* shall be such only as the opposition of moral purity to moral corruption—the destruction of error by the potency of truth—the overthrow of prejudice by the power of love—and the abolition of slavery by the spirit of repentance.

Their grievances, great as they were, were trifling in comparison with the wrongs and sufferings of those for whom we plead. Our fathers were never slaves—never bought and sold like cattle—never shut out from the light of knowledge and religion—never subjected to the lash of brutal task-masters.

But those, for whose emancipation we are striving—constituting at the present time at least one-sixth part of our countrymen,—are recognised by the law, and treated by their fellow-beings, as marketable commodities—as goods and chattels—as brute beasts; are plundered daily of the fruits of their toil without redress; really enjoying no constitutional nor legal protection from licentious and murderous outrages upon their persons; are ruthlessly torn asunder—the tender babe from the arms of its frantic mother—the heart-broken wife from her weeping husband—at the caprice or pleasure of irresponsible tyrants. For the crime of having a dark complexion, they suffer the pangs of hunger, the infliction of stripes, and the ignominy of brutal servitude. They are kept in heathenish darkness by laws expressly enacted to make their instruction a criminal offence.

These are the prominent circumstances in the condition of more than two millions of our people, the proof of which may be found in thousands of indisputable facts, and in the laws of the slave-holding States.

Hence we maintain—That in view of the civil and religious privileges of this nation, the guilt of its oppression is unequalled by any other on the face of the earth; and, therefore, that it is bound to repent instantly, to undo the heavy burden, to break every yoke, and to let the oppressed go free.

We further maintain—That no man has a right to enslave or imbrute his brother—to hold or acknowledge him, for one moment, as a piece of merchandise—to keep back his hire by fraud—or to brutalize his mind by denying him the means of intellectual, social, and moral improvement.

The right to enjoy liberty is inalienable. To invade it, is to usurp the prerogative of Jehovah. Every man has a right to his own body—to the products of his own labour—to the protection of law—and to the common advantages of society. It is piracy to buy or steal a native African, and subject him to servitude. Surely the sin is as great to enslave an American as an African.

Therefore we believe and affirm—That there is no difference, *in principle*, between the African slave trade and American slavery—That every American citizen, who retains a human being in involuntary bondage, as his property, is [according to Scripture*] a man stealer—That the slaves ought instantly to be set free, and brought under the protection of law—That if they had lived from the time of Pharaoh down to the present period, and had been entailed through successive generations, their right to be free could never have been alienated, but their claims would have constantly risen in solemnity—That all those laws which are now in force, admitting the right of slavery, are therefore before God utterly null and void; being an audacious usurpation of the Divine prerogative, a daring infringement on the law of Nature, a base overthrow of the very foundations of the social compact, a complete extinction of all the relations, endearments, and obligations of mankind, and a presumptuous transgression of all the holy commandments—and that therefore they ought to be instantly abrogated.

We further believe and affirm—That all persons of colour who possess the qualifications which are demanded of others, ought to be admitted forthwith to the enjoyment of the same privileges, and the exercise of the same prerogatives, as others—That the paths of preferment, of wealth, and of intelligence, should be opened as widely to them as to persons of a white complexion.

We maintain that no compensation should be given to the planters emancipating their slaves—Because it would be a surrender of the great fundamental principle, that man cannot hold property in man—Because Slavery is a crime, and therefore it is not an article to be sold—Because the holders of slaves are not the just proprietors of what they claim; freeing the slaves is not depriving them of property, but restoring it to its right owners; it is not wronging the master, but righting the slave—restoring him to himself—Because immediate and general emancipation would only destroy nominal, not real property; it would not amputate a limb or break a bone of the slaves, but by infusing motives into their breasts would make them doubly valuable to the masters as free labourers; and, because, if compensation is to be given at all, it should be given to the outraged and guiltless slaves, and not to those who have plundered and abused them.

We regard, as delusive, cruel, and dangerous, any scheme of expatriation which pretends to aid, either directly or indirectly, in the emancipation of the slaves, or to be a substitute for the immediate and total abolition of slavery.

We fully and unanimously recognise the sovereignty of each State, to legislate exclusively on the subject of slavery which is tolerated within its limits: we concede that Congress, *under the present national compact*, has no right to interfere with any of the slave States, in relation to this momentous subject.

But we maintain that Congress has a right, and is solemnly bound to suppress the domestic slave trade between the several States, and to abolish slavery in those portions of our territory which the Constitution has placed under its exclusive jurisdiction.

We also maintain that there are, at the present time, the highest obligations resting upon the people of the free States, to remove slavery by moral and political action, as prescribed in the Constitution of the United States. They are now living under a pledge of their tremendous physical force to fasten the galling fetters of tyranny upon the limbs of millions in the Southern States; they are liable to be called at any moment to suppress a general insurrection of the slaves: they authorize the slave owner to vote for three-fifths of his slaves as property, and thus enable him to perpetuate his oppression; they support a standing army at the South for its protection; and they seize the slave who has escaped into their territories, and send him back to be tortured by an enraged master or a brutal driver. This relation to slavery is criminal and full of danger: it must be broken up.

These are our views and principles—these, our designs and measures. With entire confidence in the over-ruling justice of God, we plant ourselves upon the Declaration of our Independence and the truths of Divine Revelation as upon the everlasting rock.

We shall organize Anti-Slavery Societies, if possible, in every city, town, and village in our land.

We shall send forth Agents to lift up the voice of remonstrance, of warning, of entreaty, and of rebuke.

We shall circulate, unsparingly and extensively, anti-slavery tracts and periodicals.

We shall enlist the pulpit and the press in the cause of the suffering and the dumb.

We shall aim at a purification of the churches from all participation in the guilt of slavery.

We shall encourage the labour of freemen rather than that of the slaves, by giving a preference to their productions: and

We shall spare no exertions nor means to bring the whole nation to a speedy repentance.

Our trust for victory is solely in GOD. *We* may be personally defeated, but our principles never. Truth, Justice, Reason, Humanity, must and will gloriously triumph. Already a host is coming up to the help of the Lord against the mighty, and the prospect before us is full of encouragement.

Submitting this DECLARATION to the candid examination of the people of this country, and of the friends of liberty throughout the world, we hereby affix our signatures to it; pledging ourselves that, under the guidance and by the help of Almighty God, we will do all that in us lies, consistently with this Declaration of our principles, to overthrow the most execrable system of slavery, that has ever been witnessed upon earth—to deliver our land from its deadliest curse—to wipe out the foulest stain which rests upon our national escutcheon—and to secure to the coloured population of the United States all the rights and privileges which belong to them as men, and as Americans—come what may to our persons, our interests, or our reputations—whether we live to witness the triumph of liberty, justice, and humanity, or perish ultimately as martyrs in this great, benevolent, and holy cause. Done in Philadelphia, this Sixth day of December, A. D. 1833.

*Exodus xxi. 16—Deuteronomy xxiv. 7.

Maine.
DAVID THURSTON,
NATHAN WINSLOW,
JOSEPH SOUTHWICK,
JAMES FREDERIC OTIS,
ISAAC WINSLOW.

New Hampshire.
DAVID CAMPBELL.

Vermont.
ORSON S. MURRAY.

Massachusetts.
DANIEL S. SOUTHMAYD,
EFFINGHAM L. CAPRON,
JOSHUA COFFIN,
AMOS A. PHELPS,
JOHN G. WHITTIER,
HORACE P. WAKEFIELD,
JAMES G. BARBADOES,
DAVID T. KIMBALL, Jr.
DANIEL E. JEWETT,
JOHN R. CAMBELL,
NATHANIEL SOUTHARD,
ARNOLD BUFFUM,
WILLIAM L. GARRISON.

Rhode Island.
JOHN PRENTICE,
GEORGE W. BENSON,
RAY POTTER.

Connecticut.
SAMUEL J. MAY,
ALPHEUS KINGSLEY,
EDWIN A. STILLMAN,
SIMEON S JOCELYN,
ROBERT B. HALL.

New York.
BERIAH GREEN, Jr.
LEWIS TAPPAN,
JOHN RANKIN,
WILLIAM GREEN, Jr.
ABRAAM L. COX,
WILLIAM GOODELL,
ELIZUR WRIGHT, Jr.
CHARLES W. DENISON,
JOHN FROST.

New Jersey.
JONATHAN PARKHURST,
CHALKLEY GILLINGHAM,
JOHN McCULLOUGH,
JAMES WHITE.

Pennsylvania.
EVAN LEWIS,
EDWIN A. ATLEE,
ROBERT PURVIS,
JAS. McCRUMMILL,
THOMAS SHIPLEY,
BARTH'W FUSSELL,
DAVID JONES,
ENOCH MACK,
JAMES McKIM,
AARON VICKERS,
JAMES LOUGHEAD,
EDWIN P. ATLEE,
THOMAS WHITSON,
JOHN R. SLEEPER,
JOHN SHARP, Jr.
JAMES MOTT.

Ohio.
JOHN M. STERLING,
MILTON SUTLIFF,
LEVI SUTLIFF.

The anti-slavery movement grew during the time Isabella lived in New York City. In December 1833, the Anti-Slavery Society met in Philadelphia, Pennsylvania, and wrote this declaration about what should be done to help end slavery.

The jury decided Matthias was innocent. Mr. Pierson had died naturally. Matthias left to preach elsewhere.

Isabella returned to New York City to work for Perez Whiting. She looked forward to being with Peter again.

For many African Americans, New York City was an exciting place. There were jobs. There was an African-American newspaper. There were African-American groups working hard to make life easier for the freed slaves. African Americans worked side by side with white Americans to end slavery across the country. There were schools for African-American students, too.

One of Isabella's friends said Peter "was so smart, he ought to have an education." The friend paid a fee of $10 for him to go to navigation school to learn to guide ships. Then he could get a good job.

For two years Peter tricked Isabella. He pretended he went to navigation school. Instead, he was dancing or doing nothing with his friends.

When Isabella learned what Peter was doing, she

gave him another chance. She got him a job as a coachman. He dressed in fine clothes and drove his employer around town. Soon Peter grew bored and sold his driving clothes.

He begged his mother to forgive him and cried "how he had *tried* to be good."

Isabella forgave him, but she wanted him to leave New York and his bad friends. She asked him to join a ship going out to sea. Peter refused.

Before long, Peter broke a law and was sent to jail. He begged his mother to get him out. She refused. Isabella wanted him to learn his lesson.

So Peter sent word to Peter Williams, a barber who was known for helping people in trouble. Mr. Williams said he would get Peter out of jail, but he had to promise to sail on a whaling ship the next week.

Peter agreed.

Two years later Isabella received a letter from Peter dated October 17, 1840.

I . . . write to you . . . that I am well, and in hopes to find you the same. I am . . . so far from your home, in the wide, briny [salty] sea. I have seen more of the world than I ever expected. . . . Mother, I hope you do not forget me, your dear and only son. I hope you all will forgive me for all that I have done.

Isabella received two more letters from Peter. In his last letter dated September 19, 1841, he wrote, "When this you see, remember me, and place me in your mind."

This was the last Isabella ever heard from the son she had fought so desperately to free from slavery. She never knew what happened to him.

Isabella felt alone in New York. Her daughters lived eighty miles away. Her husband, Tom, had died. Peter was gone.

What would she do now? Once again Isabella prayed. God told her "to go East."

Her life took a new direction.

SOJOURNER TRUTH

ISABELLA DECIDED TO LEAVE NEW YORK. She knew she had strong speaking powers. She would travel the countryside telling folks about God.

On June 1, 1843, Isabella once again packed her few belongings in a pillowcase. She put food in a small basket. She told her employer, Mrs. Whiting, that she was leaving.

She told Mrs. Whiting that her name was no longer Isabella. Her name now was Sojourner. She would be a traveler for God.

Mrs. Whiting asked her to please stay. Sojourner said no. God told her "to go East" and east she would go.

Mrs. Whiting asked, "What are you going east for?"

Sojourner answered, "The Spirit calls me there, and I must go." She would speak to people, telling them about "the hope that was in her."

Sojourner took the ferry east to Brooklyn, New York, which was on Long Island. She walked east all day. That day someone asked her name. She replied, "Sojourner." Then she realized she needed a last name.

As Belle and Isabella, Sojourner had never had her own last name. She had taken the names of her masters.

Sojourner said, "I told the Lord I wanted another name 'cause everybody else had two names. And the Lord gave me Truth, because I was to declare the truth to the people."

She would be Sojourner Truth.

Sojourner Truth did not worry about food or shelter. She worked to get a little money and then traveled on. At night, she asked for a place to sleep.

As she traveled, Sojourner went to religious

meetings where people spoke about God. Sojourner shared her views. She had a strong voice and could be heard in a large crowd. She had a message to share about her life and her love of God.

Soon Sojourner held meetings of her own. She spoke "to large audiences, having a good time."

Sojourner's rich, low voice captivated people. A friend wrote that Sojourner was a "great favorite at our meetings, both on account of her remarkable gift in prayer, and still more remarkable talent for singing."

Sojourner sang songs people already knew. She also made up many songs. One of her favorites was called "It Was Early in the Morning."

It was early in the morning,
It was early in the morning,
Just at the break of day
When He rose—when He rose—when He rose,
And went to heaven on a cloud.

After crossing Long Island, Sojourner took a ferry to Bridgeport, Connecticut. She preached, worked to get money, and walked to New Haven, Connecticut. There she spoke at many meetings before once again moving on.

As Sojourner traveled, she listened to other preachers. She discussed religion with them. Since she could not read, she enjoyed having the Bible read to her.

Sojourner liked having a child read to her more than an adult. If she asked an adult to read something a second time, the adult usually tried to explain it to her. Sojourner liked children reading the Bible to her because "children would reread the same sentence to her, as often as she wished, and without comment."

At one meeting, Sojourner was in danger. Some young men tried to break up the meeting by waving wooden clubs and shouting at the speakers. Sojourner ran into a tent and hid. She thought, "I am the only colored person here, and on me, probably, their wicked mischief will fall first."

Sojourner changed her mind. "Have I not faith enough to go out and quell [stop] that mob when I

Sojourner Truth became a traveling preacher in 1843. She was forty-six years old.

know it is written [in the Bible] 'One shall chase a thousand, and two put ten thousand to flight.'"

She left her hiding place saying, "The Lord shall go with and protect me." She said, "I felt as if I had *three hearts!* and they were so large, my body could hardly hold them."

The main speaker trembled before the gang of shouting bullies.

Sojourner walked to a small hill and began singing "It was early in the morning..."

The young men rushed at her, waving their torches and clubs. Sojourner asked, "Why do you come about me with clubs and sticks? I am not doing harm to any one."

One bully answered, "We ar'n't going to hurt you, old woman. We came to hear you sing."

Someone asked her to climb on a wagon so more could hear. Sojourner said, "If I do, they'll overthrow it."

The chief of the gang said, "He who dares hurt you, we'll knock him down instantly."

Sojourner climbed onto a wagon. She sang and

preached. After a long time she grew tired. Exhausted, she asked, "If I sing one more hymn for you, will you then go away, and leave us this night in peace?"

A few said, "Yes."

"I repeat it," Sojourner said, "and I want an answer from you all."

More bullies said, "Yes, yes, yes."

Sojourner asked her question a third time.

"Yes! Yes!" roared the bullies.

"AMEN! It is SEALED," said Sojourner. She sang another beautiful song "in the deepest and most solemn tones of her powerful voice."

When she finished, only a few of the gang left.

Sojourner sang them another song. All at once, like "a swarm of bees," the bullies rushed away.

Sojourner, a lone black woman, had faced down a gang. Her rich voice, wonderful songs, and life story had won them over.

Never again would Sojourner Truth be frightened by anyone. She had a message to share, and share it she would, no matter what obstacles came her way.

CHAPTER 10

THE NARRATIVE

SOJOURNER'S FOOTSTEPS FOUND HER in Northampton, Massachusetts, in the winter of 1843. She heard about a group of men, women, and children who lived a simple life. They had purchased a factory where they were spinning silk to make cloth.

Sojourner went to visit. She saw educated people trying to live a good life without harming anyone. The group shared everything. Both men and women had the same rights. Women spoke up in meetings. They voted in group decisions.

This was very different from anything Sojourner had ever experienced. Usually, a man had the rights and a woman had little if any voice in decisions. A husband owned the property, even that which might have once belonged to his wife.

Especially appealing to Sojourner, the group was against slavery.

Sojourner said, "Well, if these [people] can live here, I can."

She joined the sixty-five members of the Northampton Association of Education and Industry. Immediately, Sojourner added her talents to the group. She saw that the members' clothing had not been properly washed. She quickly became the leader of the laundry workers. She sang, talked about religion, and worked hard.

Here Sojourner raised her voice against slavery. Many famous speakers and writers came to visit the group. One was William Lloyd Garrison, the outspoken leader of the abolitionists who fought to end slavery in the United States. Garrison spoke against slavery whenever he could. His weekly newspaper, *The Liberator,* was read out loud at meetings.

Sojourner met the former slave Frederick Douglass

Sojourner Truth was the head laundry worker of the Northampton Association of Education and Industry from 1843 to 1846.

of Maryland. Douglass stood tall and his eyes shone with intensity when he spoke against slavery. In 1845, Douglass wrote the story of his life in a book called *The Narrative of the Life of Frederick Douglass, An American Slave*. The book became very popular and opened many Americans' eyes to the horrors of slavery in the Southern states.

Parker Pillsbury, another famous abolitionist, came to Northampton. He had been a minister. He wanted people to fight slavery everywhere. He quit his church and roamed New England urging others to join the battle.

Then, in 1846, the Northampton Association ran into trouble. The silk factory went out of business. The community broke up. Once again, Sojourner was on her own.

She fondly remembered her years with the Northampton Association. "I was with them heart and soul for anything concerning human right.... What good times we had."

Sojourner went to work for George Benson, one of the Northampton Association founders.

Sam Hill had also belonged to the Northampton Association. He wanted Sojourner to stay in Northampton, so he offered to build Sojourner her own house. Was her dream finally to come true? Would she really have a home to call her own?

Sojourner agreed to let Mr. Hill build the home, but she insisted on paying for it herself. He agreed to let her pay $300 when she could. Sojourner signed the ownership papers with an X for her name.

But where would she get $300?

Sojourner met Olive Gilbert during this time. Olive Gilbert urged Sojourner to write her own narrative that would tell the story of her life. Frederick Douglass's *Narrative* was earning him money. His book was a powerful voice against slavery. Other narratives spoke about slavery, but these had been written by men who had been Southern slaves.

Sojourner's story would be different. She was a woman. And she had been a Northern slave.

Their friend William Lloyd Garrison eagerly agreed to publish the book. Sojourner insisted on paying for it.

Sojourner told her life story to Olive Gilbert, who wrote it down. In 1850, William Garrison printed the *Narrative of Sojourner Truth, A Northern Slave*.

When her book was published, Sojourner's hair was turning gray. She was fifty-three years old. She wore glasses to help her see her work. The years of hard labor and travel were taking their toll on her.

To pay for her house and the book, Sojourner took to the road. She walked the countryside preaching, singing, and selling her *Narrative*.

SPEAKING OUT

SOJOURNER TRUTH BEGAN HER HARDEST work against slavery in 1850. It was a good year for her to speak out. In that year Congress passed the Fugitive Slave Act. A fugitive was a slave who ran away from his or her master. Before this, if a slave escaped from the South and reached the free states of the North, he or she could live in freedom.

The Fugitive Slave Act changed this. The Act made it legal for people to track down runaway slaves, even in free states. Rewards were given to people who caught slaves and returned them to their masters.

Sojourner Truth, William Garrison, Frederick Douglass, and other abolitionists spoke against the law. Groups were organized to protect freed slaves that were already living in the North. The Underground Railroad grew. The Underground Railroad was not a real railroad. It was the name for the people and pathways that slaves used to flee the South.

The abolitionists held meetings. These meetings were an excellent place for Sojourner to sell her *Narrative*. William Garrison told the audience who she was and urged them to buy her book.

One day William Garrison asked Sojourner to speak to his audience. She worried about what she would say, especially because a famous abolitionist, Wendell Phillips, would speak after her.

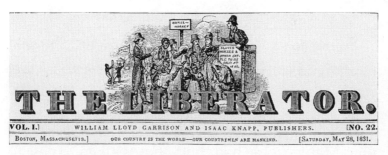

Abolitionist newspapers like William Garrison's The Liberator *ran articles opposing the Fugitive Slave Act.*

"I thought, I can do one thing that he can't do....
So I said I had a home-made song that I wanted to
sing."

Taking a deep breath, she sang one of her own
songs in her rich, powerful voice.

> *I am pleading for my people,*
> *A poor downtrodden race*
> *Who dwell in freedom's boasted land*
> *With no abiding place.*

> *I am pleading for the mothers*
> *Who gaze in wild despair*
> *Upon the hated auction-block*
> *And see their children there.*

Sojourner was a big success that night. She sold
many books. Later, she sold her songs for five and
ten cents.

She also sold her own picture. Photography was
new. Many people had their photos taken to give to
friends. Sojourner decided to sell her picture. This

way she could earn money and help spread her antislavery message.

Sojourner called her pictures her "shadow." Many of her pictures had these words printed on the bottom: "I sell the shadow to support the substance." She sold her shadow so she could pay her debts and continue her work.

In October 1850, Sojourner's life took another turn. She was invited to attend a national Women's Rights Convention in Worcester, Massachusetts. Sojourner was eager to go.

At the convention she found many abolitionist friends. Frederick Douglass, William Garrison, Wendell Phillips, Lucretia Mott, and others were there to speak for women's rights. Sojourner was the only African-American woman present.

Not everyone was in favor of this meeting. One newspaper called the convention a "motley mingling of abolitionists" and other troublemakers. This did not stop the meeting.

Sojourner spoke to the group. She said women had a responsible role to play in the world. The

I SELL THE SHADOW TO SUPPORT THE SUBSTANCE.

SOJOURNER TRUTH.

Sojourner Truth sold photos like this one when she made speeches.

New York Herald newspaper wrote Sojourner Truth "contended for her right to vote, to hold office, to practice medicine and the law, and to wear the breeches [pants] with the best white man that walks on God's earth."

In Providence, Rhode Island, in November 1850, Sojourner spoke against the hated Fugitive Slave Act. She said that "the worst had to come worst" meaning the slave law was wrong. But she also said, "the best must come to best." She urged good Americans to fight the law.

In December, Sojourner spoke in Plymouth, Massachusetts. She shared the platform with William Garrison. There she made a new friend, George Thompson from England. Thompson was a member of Parliament, Britain's lawmaking body. He had worked hard to end slavery in that country.

Sojourner sold her book at the meeting. Afterward, Thompson invited her to join him and Garrison on a lecture tour. Together they would speak against slavery and she could sell more books.

Later, Sojourner told Garrison, "My heart is

glowing now with the remembrance of his [George Thompson's] kindness to me in 1851."

The pair had planned to meet in Springfield, Massachusetts, in January 1851. Sojourner traveled there, but was disappointed to learn that Garrison was sick and could not come. Mr. Thompson greeted her "as if I had been the highest lady in the land." He asked her if she still wanted to go. She did, but she had no money.

Mr. Thompson said, "I'll bear your expenses, Sojourner. Come with us!"

She did. Throughout February and March, Sojourner and her companions traveled and spoke against slavery.

When the tour ended in Rochester, New York, Sojourner had influenced many lives. Her speeches were warm, witty, and wise. She expressed concern for slaves and made others feel concern as well.

One friend wrote: "She possesses a mind of rare power, and often, in the course of her short speeches, will throw out gems of thought."

With her increasing popularity, Sojourner found

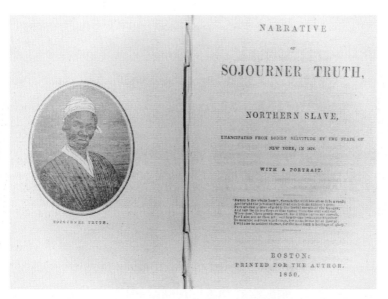

Sojourner Truth used the money she earned from the sale of her book to pay for her house in Northampton, Massachusetts, and to support herself.

it easier to sell her book. She finally had a home, but was now too busy to enjoy it. Still, she saved her money to pay off her debts.

In Rochester, Sojourner made two new friends, Amy and Isaac Post. The Posts guided many escaped slaves on the Underground Railroad, which stretched from the Southern states to Canada's borders. The Posts and other Underground Railroad conductors helped the runaway slaves find freedom in Canada. Canada did not allow slavery. Once a slave reached Canada, he or she was legally free. No one could force a slave to return to his or her master.

One of Sojourner's favorite songs was about going to Canada. It was a song sung by Harriet Tubman, an escaped slave, who led hundreds of other runaway slaves to freedom.

> *I'm on my way to Canada,*
> *That cold, but happy land:*
> *The dire* [awful] *effects of slavery*
> *I can no longer stand.*

Sojourner stayed with the Posts for three months after the lecture tour ended. Then Sojourner decided to tour on her own. First, she would attend another national Women's Rights Convention. This convention opened on May 28, 1851, in an Akron, Ohio, church.

Here Sojourner made her most memorable speech.

AIN'T I
A WOMAN?

BOTH WOMEN AND MEN ATTENDED the Women's Rights Convention in Akron, Ohio. Many people spoke about the need to change laws so women could own property. Others asked for women to have the right to vote in elections. Once again Sojourner was the only African-American woman to attend.

The first speeches began. Sojourner sat on the steps leading up to the pulpit where the speakers stood. In her plain clothes and white bandanna, she listened intently. Finally, she asked to address the audience, too.

Marius Robinson, a friend of Sojourner's, wrote a report about the convention. He said,

"One of the most unique and interesting speeches of the Convention was made by Sojourner Truth." He explained how it was hard to put down on paper the power of her talk.

Sojourner began her speech by saying, "I am [for] a woman's rights. I have as much muscle as any man and can do as much work as any man. I have plowed and reaped and husked and chopped and mowed."

She continued, "You [men] need not be afraid to give us our rights for fear we will take too much."

She ended her speech warning men that women must have their rights.

Sojourner was a great success. People gathered around her. Frances Gage, in charge of the convention, wrote, "Hundreds rushed up to shake hands and congratulate the glorious old mother."

A reporter for Garrison's *Liberator* wrote, "Sojourner Truth spoke in her own peculiar style, showing that she was a match for most men."

Sojourner's Akron speech is often called her "Ain't I a Woman?" speech. This story is based on an account of her speech written by Frances Gage in

1863, more than twelve years after the talk.

In Francis Gage's version, Sojourner says, "I have plowed, and planted, and gathered into barns, and no man could head [beat] me and ar'n't I a woman? I could work as much as a man, and bear the lash as well—and ar'n't I a woman?"

Many famous activists such as Elizabeth Cady Stanton (above), attended the Women's Rights Convention in Akron, Ohio, in 1851.

Mrs. Gage was a writer and a poet. It seems likely that she created the words *Ain't I a Woman?* from the antislavery motto "Am I not a Woman and a Sister?"

Whether or not Sojourner actually said "Ain't I a Woman?" is a question for history to decide. Her powerful voice and her strong message, however, convinced her listeners to believe in her. She was a hardworking woman who deserved the same rights as any man.

After the convention Sojourner sent a letter to her good friend Amy Post. Sojourner said, "On Tuesday [I] went to Akron to the Convention where I found plenty of kind friends, just like you."

She was such a success that she received invitations to speak to other groups. "They gave me so many kind invitations I hardly knew which to accept first."

Sojourner's speech was not her only success there. "I sold a good many books at [the] Convention," she told Amy Post.

In August 1851, Sojourner had someone write a letter to William Garrison. She asked for more books to be sent to her in Ohio. She told him she had sent money for her house to Mr. Hill.

Sojourner planned to stay with friends in Ohio for the winter. Her home in Northampton would sit empty while she traveled in Ohio, Indiana, New York, and Michigan.

A HOME AT LAST

S OJOURNER TRAVELED, SPEAKING AGAINST slavery and for women's rights. One writer said Sojourner was "sowing the seeds of truth in the hearts of the people." She worked to help the poor and to help people stop drinking alcohol.

Although she loved traveling, having a house had long been Sojourner's dream. She wanted her family to be together. In 1850, two of her daughters, Sophia and Diana, had come to live with Sojourner in Northampton, Massachusetts. Sophia soon left to get married to Tom Schuyler. Diana stayed. She took in laundry to earn money.

Another daughter, Elizabeth, had married,

In 1850 Sojourner Truth's daughter Diana (above) moved to Northampton, Massachusetts.

moved to New Bedford, Massachusetts, and had a son named Sammy Banks.

But Sojourner was still traveling and speaking about the causes she believed in. She had a home now, but her "business" as she called it would not often let her be in Northampton.

In 1853, Diana got sick with a lung disease. Sojourner said in a letter, "My daughter Diana was laying dangerously ill at my home in Northampton." Sojourner hurried there. Elizabeth also came to nurse her sister. Diana got better.

Sojourner worked so hard selling her book that on November 1, 1854, she paid off what she owed on her home. For the first time in her life, Sojourner Truth owned a home without owing anybody any money. She was even doing well enough to buy an empty lot next to her house.

But she did not have time to enjoy her home. Her speeches kept her on the road.

Between 1850 and 1860, tensions between Southern and Northern states were running high. In the Southern states, slavery was still allowed. In the

Northern states, slavery had ended. Another big problem was the growth of the United States. New states wanted to join the Union. The question facing the country was whether the new states would allow slavery or not.

The Fugitive Slave Act added to bitter feelings. Slave owners did not want to lose their property. Abolitionists wanted all slaves in the United States to be set free.

In 1851, Harriet Beecher Stowe published a book, which became very popular and further increased tensions. Her novel, *Uncle Tom's Cabin*, was about slavery and its horrors. It made many Americans decide to work to end slavery. In 1853, Sojourner visited Harriet Beecher Stowe in Andover, Massachusetts. Mrs. Stowe wrote a magazine article about Sojourner that made Sojourner even more famous across America.

As Sojourner spoke against slavery, she asked people to believe that God would end slavery. She did not ask people to fight to end slavery. During a speech in New York in 1853, she said she did "not

This announcement for the novel Uncle Tom's Cabin *appeared in 1852.*

want any man to be killed" in working for equal rights for all.

In 1856, Sojourner's travels took her to Battle Creek, Michigan. This small village was a major stop on the Underground Railroad. Sojourner found many people in Battle Creek who supported her views. She decided to sell her home in Massachusetts where she rarely even visited. She would buy a home in Harmonia, Michigan, near Battle Creek. On September 3, 1857, Sojourner sold her Northampton home for $740 and moved to Michigan.

In 1860, her daughter Elizabeth and her grandson Sammy came to live with her. Sammy was a bright and eager eight-year-old. He helped his grandmother by reading and writing for her. Later, Diana, her husband James Corbin, and Sophia moved to Battle Creek with their families to be with Sojourner.

From her new home in Harmonia, Sojourner often went to Indiana. She felt the settlers there needed her help in fighting slavery. Her views sometimes got her into trouble. Sometimes she wasn't allowed to speak. Sometimes she was threatened. One time a man in the audience said she wasn't even a woman but a man in disguise. In her own way, she convinced him that she was indeed a woman.

Parker Pillsbury, an abolitionist friend, wrote this

about Sojourner in 1858: "The wondrous experiences of that most remarkable woman [Sojourner] would make a library.... I never saw her when she did not scatter her enemies ... winning more than victory in every battle."

Her biggest battles were yet to come. In 1860, Abraham Lincoln was elected president. Southern states had threatened to leave the Union if he were elected. By March 4, 1861, seven Southern states had left the United States to form a new nation, the Confederate States of America.

President Lincoln said they could not do this. The Confederate States did not listen. They said they would go to war rather than give in to the United States government.

On April 12, 1861, Southern troops fired on Fort Sumter in the harbor of Charleston, South Carolina. The Civil War had begun.

Many people thought the war would last only a few months. No one realized that it would go on for four long, bloody years.

Sojourner still spoke out against slavery. Her life

The Civil War began on April 12, 1861 when soldiers from the South fired upon Fort Sumter in South Carolina.

was threatened. Her friends asked her to carry a weapon. She answered, "I carry no weapon. The Lord will [save] me without weapons. I feel safe in the midst of my enemies."

Some of Sojourner's friends such as Parker Pillsbury and William Lloyd Garrison did not believe that fighting the Civil War was the way to end slavery. They wished for a more peaceful solution.

Although Sojourner had not wanted war, when it came she backed President Lincoln. She said that if she were "ten years younger" (she was sixty-four) she "would fly to the battlefield and nurse and cook for the Massachusetts troops, brave boys! and if it came to the pinch, put in a blow, now and then."

Sojourner put her energy into her causes. She encouraged free black men to join the Union Army. When her grandson James Caldwell joined, she proudly blessed him. He was going to save "white people from the curse [slavery] that God has sent upon them."

James told her, "Now is our time, Grandmother, to prove that we are men."

Sojourner helped out at a training camp for African-American soldiers in Detroit. She asked friends in Battle Creek to donate food, which she delivered to the soldiers. At the camp she gave a speech encouraging the African-American soldiers to fight hard.

Sojourner still loved to sing. She made up songs for the African-American soldiers. She sang this song to the tune of "The Battle Hymn of the Republic."

Father Abraham [Lincoln] *has spoken, and the*
   message has been sent;
The prison doors have opened, and out the prisoners
   went
To join the sable [black] *army of African descent,*
As we go marching on.

On January 1, 1863, President Lincoln issued the Emancipation Proclamation. This great statement freed all slaves in states fighting against the United States.

Many freed slaves went to Washington, D.C. In 1864, Sojourner decided to join them. She wanted "to see the freedmen of my people. This is a great and glorious day."

In Washington, Sojourner worked at a camp for freed slaves. She gave talks and taught homemaking skills there. Captain George Carse, the person in charge of the camp, wrote that Sojourner "urged them [freed slaves] to embrace for their children all opportunities of education and advancement...."

She goes into their cabins…and while she talks, she knits."

Sojourner's fourteen-year-old grandson Sammy went with her to the camp. He helped with her work. He read newspapers to the freed slaves so they knew what was happening in the war. They especially wanted news about President Lincoln, the man who had freed them.

Sojourner wanted to know about him, too. So she decided to visit President Lincoln at the White House.

PRESIDENT
LINCOLN

ON OCTOBER 29, 1864, SOJOURNER went to see President Lincoln. She took her Book of Life. It contained signatures of people that she admired. She pasted in newspaper articles about her life and speeches, too.

Sojourner told a friend, "It was about eight o'clock, A.M. when I called on the President." She had to wait three hours until he finished his war work.

"The President was seated at his desk....He then arose, gave me his hand, made a bow, and said, 'I am pleased to meet you.'"

Sojourner told him she had been worried when

Sojourner Truth met President Abraham Lincoln at the White House on October 29, 1864.

he was elected. "Mr. President, when you first took your seat I feared you would be torn to pieces [by his enemies]." She was glad he had been spared. She said, "I appreciate you, for you are the best President who has ever taken the seat."

President Lincoln told her other men had been good presidents, especially George Washington. Sojourner said, "I thank God that you were the instrument selected by Him and the people to [lead during the Civil War]."

President Lincoln showed her a beautiful Bible given to him by the freed slaves of Baltimore. Sojourner handed him her Book of Life.

"He took my little book, and with the same hand that signed the death-warrant of slavery, he wrote as follows: *For Aunty Sojourner Truth, A. Lincoln. Oct. 29, 1864.*"

Sojourner said, "I must say, and I am proud to say, that I never was treated by any one with more kindness and cordiality [politeness] than were shown to me by that great and good man, Abraham Lincoln."

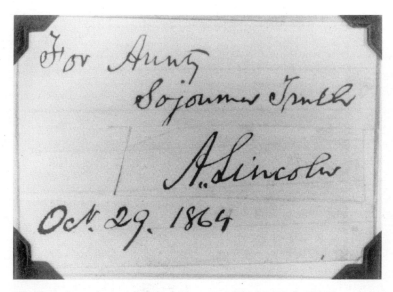

Abraham Lincoln autographed Sojourner Truth's Book of Life.

There is another story about Sojourner's visit to Lincoln. She told it in a speech she made in 1869. "I told him [Lincoln] that I had never heard of him before he was talked of for president."

He smilingly replied, "I had heard of you many times before that."

The Civil War ended on April 9, 1865. A week later, on April 15, President Lincoln died after being shot. The country grieved for its fallen leader.

Although Sojourner was saddened by Lincoln's death, she still devoted herself to her work. She also fought for the rights of African Americans.

Before he had died, President Lincoln signed a law saying that African Americans could ride on streetcars in Washington, D.C. Before this they were not allowed on the horse-drawn cars with white people.

Many African Americans did not ride the streetcars. For those who did, rides were often unpleasant. Sometimes white riders made fun of them or moved to other seats to get away from them. Sojourner believed this was wrong and set out to correct it.

One day Sojourner was with her white friend Laura Haviland. Laura signaled for a streetcar to stop. The conductor thought only Laura was getting on. Instead Sojourner "jumped aboard" ahead of her.

The conductor threatened to throw Sojourner off. She refused.

"I'll put you off," he said furiously. He grabbed Sojourner's right arm with both hands.

Laura Haviland told the conductor to leave Sojourner alone.

"Does she belong to you? If she does, take her in out of the way," he snapped.

Laura replied, "She does not belong to me, but she belongs to Humanity."

The conductor pushed Sojourner against the door. He pushed so hard she bruised her shoulder.

Sojourner complained to the owner of the streetcar company. He fired the conductor. He told Sojourner to take the man to court for hurting her.

Sojourner, who had won Peter's freedom in court long ago, agreed. Once again she won.

Her efforts to ride brought results. Soon, she said, "The inside of the cars looked like pepper and salt."

In addition to helping freed slaves better their lives, Sojourner helped them find jobs away from Washington, D.C. In 1866, she took a group of freed slaves to the Midwest to find new homes. They filled five train cars.

Sojourner placed an ad in two Rochester, New York, newspapers.

"Sojourner Truth, is now in Rochester...to find employment for some of the Southern freed people....They are willing and able to work.... Sojourner Truth, who is the life and soul of this movement, intends holding meetings...to aid this effort."

Later, she worked to bring freed slaves to Battle Creek. She bought a barn and turned it into a large house where freed slaves could live. She helped dig the cellar, carrying away dirt in her apron. She asked others to give money, having already spent most of her own.

Sojourner was more than seventy years old, but she was tireless. In 1870, she returned to Washington, D.C., to urge Congress to give land to the freed slaves. She, along with many others, believed that land out West should be given to the former slaves so they could earn their own living. Then they would not have to depend on the government for food and clothing.

Sojourner created a petition that she would take to Congress.

To The Senate and House of Representatives:
We, the undersigned, . . . earnestly request your Honorable Body [Congress] *to set apart for them* [freed slaves] *a portion of the public land in the West. . . .*

Sojourner had fifty copies printed. From February 1870 to March 1871, Sojourner and her grandson Sammy gathered signatures on her petitions. She met President Grant and had him sign her Book of Life. Sojourner paid for her travels by selling her photographs and her *Narrative*.

Congress did not listen. Sojourner said in December 1870, "Everybody says this is a good work, but nobody helps."

She went to Kansas where some freed slaves could settle. For the next two years, Sojourner and Sammy worked to find land for the freed slaves. They visited Kansas, Missouri, Iowa, and Wisconsin.

After slavery was ended, William Lloyd Garrison turned his attention to other causes like women's rights.

In 1874, Sojourner and Sammy took her petitions back to Washington, D.C. They visited friends. William Lloyd Garrison, a friend for twenty-five years, wrote that Sojourner "is indeed a remarkable woman…at her age [77] it is a pity she cannot remain quiet at her home in Battle Creek."

She would go home sooner than she expected.

Sammy got sick from an expanded blood vessel in his neck. Together they returned to Battle Creek. Sojourner cared for him until he died in February 1875. He was only twenty-four years old and had been his grandmother's constant companion.

Sojourner was tired and sick herself. In 1876, she spent two months in bed with leg problems. Some newspapers even reported that she had died.

But she hadn't. She stayed home in Battle Creek until she got better. In 1878, she made another lecture tour and returned to Rochester to visit friends. In 1880, she gave speeches in Michigan. Sojourner did not have to travel very far now. She was famous and newspapers printed reports of her speeches so Americans across the country could hear what she had to say.

Sojourner saw one of her dreams come true. Even without the help of the government, tens of thousands of freed slaves moved to Kansas. They came mostly from Tennessee, Texas, Mississippi, and Louisiana. Having worked on farms, they wanted farms of their own. Sojourner gave speeches to raise money for them. Although her own plan had not succeeded, she was excited that these freed slaves took matters in their own hands and went to Kansas.

When she was at home in Battle Creek, Sojourner had many visitors. She lived in her house on Cottage Street, where she had moved in 1867. Her home was a little "house with a background of sunflowers."

Her family was with her. Sophia visited from her home (Sojourner's old home in Harmonia) with her husband and children. Diana and her husband, James, lived with Sojourner to care for her. So did Elizabeth, whose husband had left her.

Sojourner's dreams had come true. She was free and had seen her people become free. And she owned a home with her family living close to her.

Her journey was near its end.

SOJOURNER TRUTH REMEMBERED

IN THE FALL OF 1883, SOJOURNER WAS eighty-six years old. Her legs hurt again. Dr. John Kellogg tried to cure her, but could not. He wrote a friend, "Her illness is very severe and causes her great pain. All hope is given up of a restoration [return] to health."

Sojourner knew she was at the end of her life's journey. She told her family, "I'm going home like a shooting star."

Early on November 26, 1883, Sojourner Truth died.

Her funeral was the largest ever held in Battle Creek. Her body was dressed in her simple black and white clothes. White flowers were placed in her right hand, the one she had hurt working so hard for Mr. Dumont to earn her freedom. A long line of carriages rolled to Oak Hill Cemetery where she was buried near her beloved grandson Sammy.

Frances Titus, a close friend, wrote that Sojourner had risen from slavery "and found her level among the purest and the best."

Sojourner Truth was the best-known African-American woman of her time. Born a slave, she refused to remain one. She gave her life to spread the word of God. She stood firm against slavery, speaking out against it at every opportunity. She fought to gain equal rights for all women, no matter their race.

Three years after her death, Sojourner's friend Frances Titus collected money to place a marker on Sojourner's grave.

Mrs. Titus also made certain Sojourner's story would still be told. She published a final edition of Sojourner's *Narrative*. To this book she added selections from Sojourner's Book of Life.

In 1892, Frances Titus raised money to have the artist Franklin Courter paint a picture of Sojourner's

Sojourner Truth was buried in Battle Creek, Michigan. Her friend Frances Titus collected money to pay for her grave marker.

meeting with President Lincoln. In the picture Mr. Lincoln is showing Sojourner his Bible. The painting was shown at the World Columbian Exposition in Chicago in 1893. The picture was accidentally destroyed in a fire in 1902.

In Battle Creek, Sojourner's memory continues. In 1968, May 18 was declared Sojourner Truth Day.

In 1976, an important Battle Creek highway was named for her. Scholarships are given in her honor every year.

In 1981, Sojourner was inducted into the National Women's Hall of Fame in Seneca Falls, New York. There her story is told alongside those of Susan B. Anthony, Elizabeth Cady Stanton, Lucretia Mott, and other women who fought for women's rights. In 1983, Sojourner was the first woman inducted into Michigan's Women's Hall of Fame.

In 1986, a special U.S. postage stamp was issued celebrating Sojourner's life and work. Letters carrying her image reached every part of America.

Sojourner has even gone beyond Earth. In 1997, the *Sojourner* space probe, named in her honor, was launched. Its goal was to gather information about Mars.

Today a larger-than-life-size statue of Sojourner Truth stands in Battle Creek. She gazes into the distance, toward the day when no one is enslaved, and everyone enjoys the same rights.

CHRONOLOGY

1797?   Isabella Hardenbergh is born a slave in Ulster
         County, New York.

1806   Is sold to John Neely.

1808   Is sold to Martin Schriver.

1810   Is sold to John Dumont.

1815   Marries Thomas, a fellow slave. Has five
         children: Diana (born 1815); Peter (1820);
         Elizabeth (1825); and Sophia (1826). One child
         dies as an infant.

1826   Runs away from Dumont. Goes to work for the
         Van Wagenen family.

1827   Is legally freed under New York law, which freed
         all slaves in New York who had been working for
         more than twenty years.

1828   Wins court case to free son, Peter.

1829   Moves with son, Peter, to New York City. Other
         three children remain in Ulster County.

1829–43 Lives and works in New York City.

1843   Changes her name to Sojourner Truth. Becomes
         a traveling preacher.

1844–57 Lives in Northampton, Massachusetts. Travels,
         speaking against slavery and for women's rights.

1850   The *Narrative of Sojourner Truth* is published by
         William Lloyd Garrison.

1851   Makes her famous "Ain't I a Woman?" speech in
         Akron, Ohio.

1857–83 Lives near, then in, Battle Creek, Michigan.

1864   Helps freed slaves in Washington, D.C. Meets
         President Lincoln.

1870   Meets President Grant.

1875   Grandson Sammy Banks dies at age twenty-four.

1883   (November 26) Sojourner Truth dies in Battle
         Creek, Michigan.

BIBLIOGRAPHY

Blockson, Charles L. *The Underground Railroad*. New York: Prentice Hall Press, 1987.

Davis, Ossie. *Escape to Freedom: A Play About Young Frederick Douglass*. New York: Puffin Books, 1978.

Gilbert, Olive. *Narrative of Sojourner Truth*. New York: Penguin Putnam, 1998.

Hurmence, Belinda, editor. *We Lived in a Little Cabin in the Yard*. Winston-Salem, North Carolina: John F. Blair, Publisher, 1994.

Kelley, Robin and Lewis, Earl, editors. *To Make Our World Anew: A History of African Americans*. New York: Oxford University Press, 2000.

Mabee, Carleton with Susan Mabee Newhouse. *Sojourner Truth: Slave, Prophet, Legend*. New York: New York University Press, 1993.

Painter, Nell Irvin. *Sojourner Truth: A Life, A Symbol*. New York: Norton, 1996.

Roop, Peter and Connie. *Susan B. Anthony*. Des Plaines, Illinois: Heinemann, 1998.

Sprague, Stuart. *His Promised Land*. New York: Norton, 1996.

U.S. Department of the Interior. *Underground Railroad*. Washington, D.C., 1998.

Whalin, W. Terry. *Sojourner Truth: American Abolitionist*. Philadelphia: Chelsea House, 1999.

FURTHER READING

Ferris, Jeri. *Walking the Road to Freedom*. Minneapolis: Carolrhoda Books, 1988.

Lester, Julius. *To Be a Slave*. New York: Scholastic, 1968.

McLoone, Margo. *Sojourner Truth: A Photo-Illustrated Biography*. Mankato, MN: Capstone Press, 1997.

McKissack, Patricia and Fredrick. *Sojourner Truth: Ain't I a Woman?* New York: Scholastic Paperbacks, 1994.

Rappaport, Doreen. *American Women: Their Lives in Their Words*. New York: Thomas Y. Crowell, 1990.

———. *Escape From Slavery: Five Journeys to Freedom*. New York: HarperCollins, 1991.

Shumate, Jane. *Sojourner Truth and the Voice of Freedom*. Brookfield, CT: Millbrook Press, 1991.

FOR MORE INFORMATION

Sojourner Truth Institute of Battle Creek
Battle Creek, Michigan

Sojourner's home no longer exists, but you can get a flavor of the Battle Creek of her time by walking through town. Some old buildings have been preserved and are marked with plaques. You will see the larger-than-life-sized statue of Sojourner Truth in Monument Park. Another important monument is the Underground Railroad sculpture. This work of art honors those who helped slaves escape along the Underground Railroad.

(5 Riverwalk Center, Battle Creek, MI 49017)
Phone: (616) 965-0521
Web site: www.sojournertruth.org.

National Women's Hall of Fame
Seneca Falls, New York
This informative museum covers the history of the women's movement. Displays show how women like Susan B. Anthony, Elizabeth Cady Stanton, and Sojourner Truth fought and won the battle for women's rights. There are exhibits and historical artifacts. Elizabeth Cady Stanton's home is nearby.

(76 Fall Street, Seneca Falls, NY 13146)
Phone: (315) 568-8060
Web site: www.greatwomen.org.

PHOTO CREDITS

Library of Congress: 7, 65, 86, 107; New York Historical Society: 13; North Wind Picture Archives (Alfred, ME): 16, 33, 37, 44, 47, 83, 102, 114; Surrogate's Court of Ulster Country (Kingston, NY): 21; Superstock: 25; New York Public Library (New York, NY): 28; Phyllis McCabe: 53; Kingston Senate House Museum (Kingston, NY): 56; Brown Brothers (Sterling, PA): 61, 93; University of Michigan: 5, 10, 18, 23, 31, 40, 50, 59, 69, 73, 76, 82, 89, 91, 95, 106, 109, 117, 119; Historic Northampton: 78; Willard Public Library: 96; Granger Collection: 99

INDEX

Bold numbers refer to photographs